EASY JAPANESE PICKLING
IN FIVE MINUTES
TO ONE DAY

101 Full-Color Recipes
for Authentic Tsukemono

Seiko Ogawa
Translated by Laura Driussi

CONTENTS

CHAPTER TWO
Fruit, Seafood, Meats

About the Author:

Seiko Ogawa has written several Japanese cookbooks on streamlined techniques and quick ways to make delicious meals and desserts. she is a popular guest on Japanese television shows and her recipes are regularly featured in women's magazines.

How to Use This Book (sample)

Na no Hana	·Basic Prep: Rinse with hot water, then cool. ·Also Try in: Wasabi Soy Sauce (opposite), Spicy Soy Sauce (page 42)

Marinate 10 min	Marinate 5 min	Marinate 30 min	Marinate 30 min
Plastic bag	Bowl	Dish	Jar

·As shown at right, this book provides basic prep instructions for each ingredient, plus a list of other recipes that work well for the ingredient.
·Light blue symbols show the type of container and the marinating time.
·In the recipes, 1 cup = 200cc (ML), 1 Tbsp = 15 cc (ML), 1 tsp = 5 cc (ML).
·Microwave times are for a 500-watt oven.
·When dashi (stock) is called for, use instant or homemade (with kombu and shaved bonito).
·Vinegar refers to rice wine vinegar.

Quick to make, quick to the table

Pointers for Speedy Tsukemono

In this book, you will find 130 varieties of Japanese pickles-tsukemono-that can be made in 5 minutes to 24 hours. Every tsukemono in this book is more fresh and flavorful than anything in the stores, and yet each is easy to prepare with the simple pointers shown here.

No Special Containers Needed

For tsukemono for 4 people or fewer, no special pot or press is required. Ordinary kitchen materials-plastic wrap, plastic bags, and baking dishes-work better and faster.

•Plastic Bag Pickling–Easy Cleanup

You can use a plastic bag for any tsukemono that does not use too much vinegar and is not hot. In a traditional pot, much of the time is spent waiting for the liquid level to reach the top of the ingredients. In a bag (as below), the ingredients are surrounded by the liquid from the start and quickly absorb the flavors. Plus, the bag takes up little space in the refrigerator, and there is no container to wash.

•Spare the Dish! Plastic Wrap for Misozuke

Miso-flavored pickles are traditionally pickled for 2-3 days. Instead, use paper towels and plastic wrap (opposite page, bottom) and the pickles are ready in an hour or two.

•Canned Goods Do the Heavy Work

Even for layered vegetables, a special press is not required. Just cover with plastic wrap and a small plate, then put canned goods on top.

How to Pickle with a Plastic Bag

1 Put vegetables and flavorings in a plastic bag.

2 Inflate bag slightly and shake ingredients.

3 Let stand until vegetables wilt slightly.

4 Squeeze the air out and tie the opening.

2 — Speeding Up Specialized Pickling Techniques

•Cut Small Pieces for Western-style Pickles

A modified version of Western-style pickling is now a tsukemono favorite in Japan. These "pikurusu" normally take several hours to prepare, but if the vegetables are cut into small pieces, they can be ready as soon as the vegetables are boiled and cooled.

Small bite-size pieces absorb the flavors faster.

•Use Instant Nuka for Nukazuke

Nukazuke, the method used to make takuan pickles, is one of the most popular types of tsukemono. But the traditional method, using rice lees, is difficult to learn. In this book, we add kombu and other flavorings to instant nuka (popular brands include Nuka-Doko, *right*, and Nukazuke no Moto). Vegetables that used to cure for 2-3 weeks are now ready in 1 day.

3 — Ready-Made Ingredients Save More Time

For even speedier preparations, flavor your marinades with ready-made dried foods, *right*. Choose ingredients with intense flavor and good salt content. Ready-made pickles can be used as well, such as Chinese zaasai or sweet-pickled shallots. Try some of your own favorites, too.

with dried shrimp Carrots with Shrimp (p. 52)

with smoked squid Marinated Squid (p. 52)

How to Make Misozuke with Plastic Wrap

1 Spread miso on the wrap.

2 Cover with paper towel. Spread vegetables.

3 Cover with another paper towel.

4 Spread miso. Fold wrap. Place in plastic bag.

*Note: The miso can be reused several times.

Simple and Speedy
Tsukemono in 30 Minutes or Less

Perfect for the accompaniment to a quick meal.

Simple! Only two ingredients!

Nappa with Kombu

Marinate
25 min

[4 servings]
¼ head nappa or hakusai
1 Tbsp kombu tea powder (low salt)

1. Slice leaves off stalks and chop. Slice stalks against the grain into ¼ in-wide (7 mm) strips.
2. Put stalk strips in a plastic bag. Sprinkle with kombu. Let soften 5-7 min.
3. Stir in the leaves. Squeeze out the air and tie the bag. Let stand 20-30 min.

Use your favorite variety of mushrooms

Sautéed Mushrooms

Marinate
Til cool

[4 servings]
1 pack eringi mushrooms
6 large fresh shiitake
2 packs enoki mushrooms
1 dried chile

3 Tbsp soy sauce
2 Tbsp vinegar
2 Tbsp sake
4 Tbsp cooking oil

1. Chop mushrooms. Seed chile. Mix soy sauce and vinegar in a large bowl.
2. Heat oil and chile in a pan. When hot, sauté the eringi and shiitake, then stir in the enoki.
3. Add sake. Pour mushroom mixture into soy sauce mixture. Let cool.
*Can also be made a day ahead.

The plastic bag seals in the bonito flavor

Tosa-style Cucumbers

Marinate
10 min

[4 servings]
4 cucumbers
⅓ oz (10 g) shaved bonito

1-1½ Tbsp soy sauce

1. Slice cucumbers into ⅕ in-thick (5-6 mm) diagonal rounds. Place in a plastic bag and sprinkle with bonito (*fig 1*).
2. Add soy sauce. Tie bag tightly (*fig 2*). Let stand 20-30 min, inverting occasionally.

Salted plums complement turnips

Ume Turnips

Marinate
5 min

[4 servings]
5 turnips
1 Tbsp mirin

2 umeboshi (pickled plums)

1. Peel and dice the turnips.
2. Seed the umeboshi and mince. Stir in the mirin.
3. Add the turnips (*fig*). Let stand 5 min.

Slice in half to shorten marinating time

Sweet Myoga

Marinate
30 min

[4 servings]
6 myoga (Japanese ginger)
3 Tbsp vinegar
1 Tbsp mirin

2½ Tbsp sugar
½ tsp salt

1. Dissolve the sugar and salt in the mirin and vinegar.
2. Halve the myoga lengthwise. Rinse in boiling water.
3. Drain well. Place in a bowl with the vinegar mixture. Let stand 30 min.

Easy Vegetable Tsukemono

Arranged by vegetable

Tsukemono made at home with seasonal vegetables has a depth of flavor that no store-bought tsukemono can match. On the pages that follow, we'll introduce you to some very fast, simple, and yet delicious varieties.

Spring • Summer

Cabbage

- Basic Prep:
  Blanch, sauté, or rub with salt.
- Also Try in:
  blanched Sweet Yukari (p. 11)
  salt-rubbed Kombu-zuke (p. 14)

Olive Oil Marinade

Marinate
Til cool

[4 servings]
9 oz (250 g) red cabbage · 3 Tbsp vinegar · 3 Tbsp olive oil · 1 Tbsp sugar · 2 tsp soy sauce · Dash pepper

1. Julienne cabbage. Blanch and drain.
2. Mix remaining ingredients well.

3. Toss the cabbage in the vinegar mixture. Let stand until cool.

*Be sure to drain cabbage very well before marinating.

Sauerkraut Style

Marinate
1+hr

[4 servings] 10 oz (300 g) cabbage · 1 Tsp salt · 1 Tbsp white wine · 1 Tbsp lemon juice · 1 Tsp honey · Caraway seeds · Pepper

1. Core the cabbage and julienne. Sprinkle with the salt. Mix the liquids.
2. When cabbage softens, squeeze out the liquid. Stir in caraway, pepper, and wine mixture.
Let stand 1 hour or more.

*Try serving with German sausages.

Spicy-Sweet Style

Marinate
Til cool

[4 servings] 300 g cabbage · 2 Tbsp dried shrimp · ½ naganegi, or white part of 2 scallions · 3 Tbsp vinegar · 3 Tbsp soy sauce · 1 Tbsp sugar · 2 Tbsp sesame oil · 2 Tbsp cooking oil · ½ dried chile, seeded · 2 Tbsp sake

1. Soak dried shrimp in warm water. Drain, reserving 2 Tbsp of water.
2. Core cabbage and chop. Slice scallions thinly on the diagonal.
3. Combine vinegar, soy sauce, sugar, and oil.
4. Fry chile slowly in the oil until fragrant. Add cabbage, scallions, and shrimp and sauté briefly on high. Add reserved soaking water and sake.
5. Stir cabbage mixture into vinegar mixture. Let stand until cool.

*The hot mixture absorbs the marinade quickly.

Hakata Style

Marinate
30+min

[6 servings] 400 g cabbage · 2 tsp salt · 2-3 Tbsp water · ½ carrot · 30 shiso leaves

1. Core cabbage and slice to fit a small rectangular container. Soften, sprinkled with the salt and water, 15-20 min.
2. Julienne the carrot.
3. Line the container with plastic wrap. Layer with well-squeezed cabbage, then shiso, then carrots. Repeat (fig 1).
4. Layer cabbage on top. Fold wrap over. Place dish(es) and can(s) (fig 2).
5. Let stand 30 min or til flavored well.
6. Gently remove. Slice through wrap into pieces.

*One medium-large can acts as the weight.

1

2

Facing page from top: Sauerkraut Style, Purple Cabbage, Hakata Style, Spicy-Sweet Style

Rape Blossoms (Na no Hana)

- **Basic Prep:**
Rinse with boiling water, then cool.
- **Also Try in:**
Wasabi Soy Sauce (opposite)
Spicy Soy Sauce (p. 42)

Kombu-Wrapped

Marinate
1 hr

[4 servings] 9 oz (250 g) rape blossoms · 1½ oz (40 g) oboro kombu (shaved kombu) · ⅔ tsp salt

1. Rinse rape blossoms; trim stems. Remove large flowers. Rinse in a strainer with boiling water (*fig 1*).
2. When cool, pat dry. Sprinkle salt.
3. When salt dissolves, wrap 3-stalk groups in kombu (*fig 2*). Pack tightly in bowl. Cover with wrap; weigh down (*fig 3*). Let stand 1-2 hours.

Fried Style

Marinate
1 hr

[4 servings] 10 oz (300 g) boiled bamboo shoot · ⅓ oz (10 g) shaved bonito · ½ cup water · 3 Tbsp sake · 2 Tbsp mirin · ¼ cup soy sauce · Cooking oil · Ki no me or other garnish

1. Boil the bonito, water, sake, and mirin briefly in a small pot. Strain into a bowl and add the soy sauce.
2. Cut top of shoot into wedges, base of shoot into quarter rounds. Pat dry.
3. Fry at 360°F (180°C) until lightly browned and surface is crisp.
4. Drain well. Add to bonito mixture while still hot (*fig*). Let stand 1-2 hours. Garnish and serve.

Bamboo Shoots

- **Basic Prep:**
Can be boiled and fried, or used as is.
- **Also Try in:**
fried Kombu Tea Fry (p. 42)

Udo	•Basic Prep: Soak in vinegar water, then boil in vinegared water. (If unavailable, try fennel or celery.) •Also Try in: Soy Sauce Marinade (p. 35); Sweet Vinegar (p. 39)

Sweet Yukari

Marinate
Til cool

[4 servings] 10 oz (300 g) udo • Vinegar for soaking, boiling • 2 Tbsp sugar • 3 Tbsp vinegar • 1 Tbsp yukari (dried beefsteak leaves) • 1½ Tbsp sake • 1½ Tbsp water

1. Peel the udo thickly and chop. Soak in vinegar water. Blanch in water with a dash of vinegar. Drain well.
2. Mix other ingredients. Add hot udo. Cool.
*Cook udo just til al dente.

Fuki (Butterbur)	•Basic Prep: Roll in salt, boil, then peel. (Substitute with celery.) •Also Try in: Misozuke (p. 24); Honey-Lemon (p. 26)

Wasabi Soy Sauce

Marinate
1 hr

[4 servings] 2 in (5 cm) kombu • ⅓ cup water • 10 oz (300 g) fuki • 1-2 Tbsp salt • 2 Tbsp mirin • 2 Tbsp sake • ¼ cup soy sauce • Wasabi root, julienned

1. Cut kombu into 5 strips; soak in the water.
2. Cut fuki to fit in pot. Sprinkle with the salt and roll on board. Blanch, starting with thick pieces. Plunge in cold water, then peel. Cut to serving length. Pat dry.

3. Boil kombu in its water. Add mirin and sake. Boil off alcohol. Cool. Add soy sauce, wasabi.
4. Place udo and kombu mixture in a plastic bag. Let stand 1-2 hours.

Cooking with Tsukemono

●using Fuki in Wasabi Soy Sauce

Tofu Steak

[2 servings] 1 block tofu (10½ oz; 300 g) • 1 oz (30 g) Fuki in Wasabi Soy Sauce, with 2 Tbsp marinade • Dash salt • 1 Tbsp cooking oil • Watercress

1. Slice tofu in half crosswise, then halve again horizontally. Line a dish with paper towels. Drain tofu on paper towels 30 min, changing towels.
2. Slice the Fuki thinly on the diagonal.
3. Salt tofu and fry both sides in the oil until crisp. Remove. Briefly

sauté Fuki and marinade. Pour over tofu. Garnish with watercress.

Bell Peppers

- Basic Prep:
Roast the skin, then seed; or use raw (cored)
- Also Try in:
roasted Chinese Style (p. 14)
roasted or sauteed Lemon Sauté (opposite)

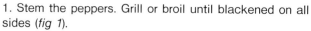

Roasted

Marinate
30 min

[4 servings] 4 bell peppers (red and yellow) · 6 Tbsp olive oil · 3 Tbsp vinegar · 1 Tbsp sugar · 1 tsp salt · Coarsely ground pepper · 3 Tbsp minced onion

1. Stem the peppers. Grill or broil until blackened on all sides (*fig 1*).
2. Plunge in cold water and peel (*fig 2*). Slice, discarding seeds. Pat dry.
3. Combine remaining ingredients. Add peppers. Chill 30 min (or up to 1 day).

Salt-Sesame

Marinate
1 hr

[4 servings] 8 small green bell peppers · 2 red bell peppers · ½ tsp salt · 2 Tbsp white roasted sesame seeds

1. Seed and julienne the peppers.
2. Place in a plastic bag with

the salt. Soften 10-15 min.
3. Add sesame seeds, squeeze and tie the bag, and let stand 1-2 hours.

Soy Sauce

Marinate
1 hr

[4 servings] 12 small green bell peppers · 3 in (8cm) kombu · 1 Tbsp sake · 3 Tbsp soy sauce

1. Seed and dice the peppers.
2. Julienne the kombu.
3. Knead the peppers, kombu, sake, and soy sauce in a plastic bag. Let stand 1-2 hours, inverting occasionally.

Celery

- Basic Prep:
Devein. Sauté briefly, blanch, or use raw.
- Also Try in:
blanched Honey-Apple (p. 20)
or blanched Soy Sauce with Jako (p. 23)

Lemon Sauté

Marinate
Til cool

[4 servings] 3 ribs celery · 1 clove garlic · 2 Tbsp lemon juice · 1 Tbsp sugar · 1 Tbsp vinegar · 1 tsp salt · Dash pepper · 2-3 thin slices lemon · 3 Tbsp cooking oil

1. Devein celery. Slice in ⅓ in (1 cm) diagonals. Halve garlic.
2. Mix other ingredients (except oil) in a bowl.
3. Heat garlic slowly in oil. When fragrant, raise heat and quickly sauté celery.
4. Add to marinade. Ready when cool, but even more flavorful in 1 day.

Misozuke

Marinate
2 hrs

[4 servings] 2 ribs celery · ¾ cup miso · 2 Tbsp mirin

1. Devein celery. Slice diagonally into 2 in (6 cm) lengths. Mix miso and mirin well.
2. Layer as on p. 5: plastic wrap, ⅓ of miso, paper towel, ½ of celery (fig 1), paper towel, ⅓ of miso, paper towel, rest of celery, paper towel, rest of miso (fig 2).
3. Wrap tightly with more plastic wrap, then let stand in a plastic bag 2-6 hrs.

1 2

Cooking with Tsukemono

● with Lemon-Sautéed Celery

Smoked-Salmon Salad

[2 servings] 4-5 Tbsp Lemon-Sautéed Celery with marinade · 5-6 slices smoked salmon · Lettuce
1. Chop salmon into bite-sized pieces. Combine with Celery and its marinade.
2. Serve in a dish lined with torn lettuce.

Cucumbers

・Basic Prep:
Soak in salted water or rub with salt. If Japanese cucumbers are unavailable, try English cucumbers (slightly larger).

・Also Try in:
raw Sesame Miso (p. 38)
salt-rubbed Salt-Sesame (p. 12)
salt-rubbed Spicy Soy Sauce (p. 33)

Chinese Style

Marinate
Til cool

[4 servings] 4 cucumbers · 1½ Tbsp salt · 2 cups water · 1 naganegi or 3 scallions · 3 dried shiitake · 1-2 dried chiles, halved and seeded · 2 Tbsp sesame oil · 3 Tbsp sake · 2 Tbsp sugar · 4 Tbsp vinegar · 3 Tbsp soy sauce

1. Score cucumbers diagonally to ⅔ depth. Repeat on other side (figs 1, 2; accordion cut). Soften 30-60 min in salted water. Squeeze well. Put in dish.
2. Cut naganegi in thin, diagonal half rounds. Soak shiitake; julienne, reserving 4 Tbsp water. Sauté naganegi, shiitake, and chile in oil.
3. Add sake, sugar, and soaking water to pan. Boil. Remove from heat. Add vinegar and soy sauce.
4. Pour naganegi mixture over the cucumbers (fig 3). Let stand til cool.

Kombu-zuke

Marinate
1 hr

[4 servings] 4 cucumbers · 2 in (5 cm) kombu · 1½ tsp salt

1. Slice cucumbers into ¾ in (2 cm) rounds. Julienne kombu with scissors.
2. Combine salt and cucumber slices in a plastic bag.
3. Add kombu (fig). Close bag. Let stand 1 hr.

Sandwich Style

Marinate
30 min

[4 servings] 4 cucumbers · 1½ tsp salt · Fresh ginger, julienned · 20 shiso leaves

1. Slice cucumbers diagonally ⅓ in (3 cm) thick. Make a deep incision in each slice (fig 1).
2. Combine with the salt in a plastic bag to soften, 10-15 min.
3. Fold some ginger into a shiso leaf and insert in an incision (fig 2).
4. Place in a bowl. Drape with plastic wrap. Weigh down with dishes. Let stand 30 min (fig 3).

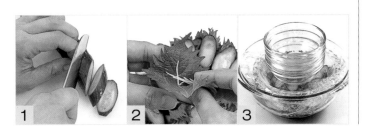

Kimchee Style

Marinate
1/2 + day

[4 servings] 5 cucumbers · 2 Tbsp salt · 7 oz (200 g) daikon · Pinch shredded carrot · Ami shiokara (salt-preserved squid innards) · 1-2 tsp cayenne pepper · 2 tsp sugar · 2-3 tsp ground sesame seeds · ½ cup juice from grated daikon · ½ cup juice from grated apple · 1 tsp juice from grated ginger

1. Halve cucumbers crosswise. Cut down the center, leaving the ends joined (fig 1). Turn and cut again, making an X.
2. Combine with the salt in a plastic bag (fig 2). Let soften 20-30 min.
3. Finely julienne the carrot and daikon. Mix well with shiokara, cayenne, sugar, and sesame (fig 3).
4. Squeeze cucumbers well. Insert the carrot mixture into the openings (fig 4).
5. Return to the plastic bag. Combine the juices and add (fig 5). Tie and let stand half a day or more.

Clockwise from top right: Kombu-zuke, Kimchee Style, Sandwich Style, Chinese Style

Steps for Kimchee Style

1	**2**	**3**	**4**	**5**
Make incisions for the filling.	Use salt to draw out the liquid.	Combine filling ingredients well.	Push in the ends to open up; fill.	Place in bag and add juice mixture.

Easy Boiled Pickles

These Western-inspired "pikurusu" are a new favorite in Japanese cuisine. Small pieces absorb the pickling juices quickly: just boil, let cool in juices, and serve.

Mixed Pickles

Marinate Til cool

[6 servings]
½ dried chile
2 Tbsp honey
1½ tsp salt
2 Tbsp sugar
½ tsp peppercorns

1 bay leaf
⅔ cup water
¾ cup vinegar
4 Japanese cucumbers
1 carrot
2 turnips
1 rib celery

1 Seed the chile. Bring honey, salt, sugar, peppercorns, bay leaf, chile, and water to a boil.

2 Let cool in a bowl. Add vinegar.

3 Peel the cucumbers in a striped pattern. Cut into ⅔ in (2 cm) rounds. Peel and chop carrot and turnips. Devein celery and chop.

4 Boil plenty of water in a pot. Add, pausing after each: carrot, then celery, then cucumber, then turnips.

5 Stir briefly, then drain well in a colander.

6 While hot, pour into the pickling liquid. Stirring occasionally, let cool. Serve when cool.

* Keeps a week to 10 days in the refrigerator.

Cooking with Tsukemono

● with Mixed Pickles

Pork Roll

[2 servings] 3 oz (80 g) Mixed Pickles · 8 thin slices pork loin · Salt and pepper · Pastry flour · 2 Tbsp cooking oil · 3-4 Tbsp liquid from Mixed Pickles · 2 tsp soy sauce · 2-3 tsp honey · 2 Tbsp butter, cut in small pieces

1. Pat Pickles dry. Julienne.
2. Lightly salt and pepper the pork slices. Roll 1/4 of the Pickles in one slice. Re-roll with a second slice. Repeat with remaining pork and Pickles.
3. Dredge lightly in flour and arrange, seam down, in heated oil. Fry on all sides until browned. Remove from heat.
4. Discard oil in pan. Boil the pickling liquid until reduced by half. Remove from heat. Stir in soy sauce and honey. Swirl butter into the sauce.
5. Pour the sauce over the pork rolls. Serve with sautéed potatoes and parsley.

More Pickles

Marmalade adds a citrus note

Kabocha Pickles

Marinate
Til cool

[4 servings] 10 oz (300 g) kabocha squash • 4 Tbsp marmalade • 4 Tbsp vinegar • 1 tsp salt

1. Mix marmalade, vinegar, and salt.
2. Slice kabocha flesh into ⅓ in-thick (1 cm) pieces. Boil until almost tender. Drain. Combine with marmalade mixture. Serve when cool.

Sweet and tart fruit from plum wine

Plum Wine Turnips

Marinate
Til cool

[4 servings] 14 oz (400 g) turnips • 2-3 plums from plum wine bottle • 4 Tbsp vinegar • 2-3 Tbsp sugar • 1 tsp salt

1. Seed the plums and mince. Combine with the vinegar, sugar, and salt.
2. Trim all but the base of the turnip leaves. Peel turnips. Quarter them from stem end. Blanch in boiling water and drain. Combine while hot with the plum mixture. Serve when cool.
* Adjust sugar depending on sweetness of plums.

Mellow eggs complement the carrots

Carrots and Quail Eggs

Marinate
Til cool

[4 servings]
2 carrots • 20 boiled quail eggs • 4 Tbsp vinegar • 4 Tbsp water • 3 Tbsp honey • 1 tsp salt • ½ tsp peppercorns • 5-6 leaves basil, torn

1. Cut carrots to match size of eggs. Boil carrots quickly, adding the shelled eggs to the water to heat a bit. Drain.
2. Mix remaining ingredients. Stir in carrots and eggs. Serve when cool.

* Carrots and Quail Eggs pickles will keep in the refrigerator 4-5 days. All other pickles on these two pages will keep 7-10 days.

White wine adds depth and richness

Fuki (Butterbur)

Marinate
Til cool

[4 servings] 10 oz (300 g) fuki (butterbur) · 1-2 Tbsp + 1 tsp salt · ¼ dried chile, seeded · ¼ cup white wine · 3 Tbsp sugar · 1 tsp salt · Dash pepper · 3 Tbsp vinegar

1. Use thin fuki stalks. (If unavailable, use celery and skip to step 2). Cut to fit pot. Rub with 1-2 Tbsp salt. Blanch, peel, slice, and pat dry.
2. Boil wine, sugar, 1 tsp salt, and pepper. Pour in bowl with vinegar.
3. Add fuki to bowl. Serve when cool.
* Be sure not to overcook the fuki.

Onions and garlic brighten the flavor

Asparagus

Marinate
2 hrs

[4 servings]
2 bunches asparagus (thin) · ¼ cup water · 2 Tbsp sugar · 1½ tsp salt · 4 Tbsp vinegar · 1 Tbsp lemon juice · ⅓ clove garlic · ¼ onion · Lemon slices

1. Blanch asparagus. Spread out in a colander to cool. Chop to bite size.
2. Boil water, sugar, salt briefly. Add vinegar and lemon juice. Thinly slice onion and garlic. Add, with lemon slices
3. Add asparagus; marinate 2-3 hours.

Ketchup and red wine meld beautifully

Pearl Onions

Marinate
Til cool

[4 servings] 14 oz (400 g) pearl onions · ½ cup ketchup · 3 Tbsp red wine · 1 Tbsp soy sauce · 2 Tbsp vinegar

1. Boil ketchup and wine. Remove from heat. Add soy sauce and vinegar.
2. Boil onions til almost tender. Drain. Let cool in ketchup mixture.

- Basic Prep:
Rub with salt or rinse with boiling water
- Also Try in:
salt-rubbed Plum Vinegared (p. 48)

Honey Apple

Marinate
30 min

[4 servings] 1½ red onions (5 oz; 150 g) · 1 tsp salt · ½ apple · 2 Tbsp lemon juice · 1½ Tbsp honey · 1 Tbsp vinegar

1. Thinly slice red onions. Sprinkle with salt and let stand 20-30 min. When softened, squeeze out all liquid.
2. Quarter apple; thinly slice crosswise. Mix with lemon juice in bowl. Mix honey and vinegar; add to bowl.
3. Stir in red onions. Let stand 30 min.

Asparagus

- Basic Prep:
Rinse with boiling water, blanch, or grill.
- Also Try in:
blanched Kombu Wrapped (p. 10) or Misozuke
(p. 23)

Kombu Tea

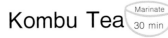
Marinate
30 min

[4 servings] ¾ lb (350 g) asparagus · 1 Tbsp instant kombu tea · 1 tsp Chinese mustard · ½ tsp soy sauce · ½ tsp mirin

1. Break off tough ends of asparagus. Blanch. Cool. Pat dry and slice diagonally.
2. Mix other ingredients. Stir in asparagus. Let stand 30 min.

Grilled

Marinate
Til cool

[4 servings] ¾ lb (350 g) asparagus, trimmed · 3 Tbsp sake · 1 Tbsp mirin · ¼ cup water · 5g shaved bonito · 1/4 cup soy sauce

1. Boil sake and mirin. Add water; return to boil. Add bonito. Remove from heat. Add soy sauce.
2. Grill or broil asparagus quickly over high heat to seal in juices.
3. Add to sake mixture while hot.

Sun-Dried Tomatoes

- **Basic Prep:**
Boil briefly, then reconstitute in chilled white wine 1-2 hours (*fig*)
- **Also Try in:**
Add to Basil Oil (p. 62)

Oil-Packed

Marinate
5+hrs

¼ lb (100 g) dried tomatoes · ½ cup white wine · ⅛ tsp oregano · 1 tsp pepper · 1 cup olive oil

1. Follow Basic Prep for tomatoes (above).
2. Let stand in a jar with other ingredients (plus olive oil to cover) 5 hours.

*Keeps 10 days in refrigerator.

*Serve whole with a bit of salt, or julienne and add to pastas or salads.

Cherry Tomatoes

- **Basic Prep:**
Stem; blanch in a slotted spoon; plunge in cold water; peel (*figs 1, 2*)
- **Also Try in:**
Honey Lemon (p. 26)

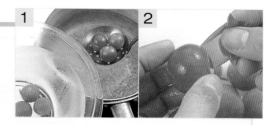

Honey Mint

Marinate
30 min

[4 servings] 10 oz (300 g) cherry tomatoes · 3 Tbsp honey · 3 Tbsp vinegar · 1 sprig mint

1. Combine honey and vinegar. Tear mint leaves into small pieces and add.
2. Follow Basic Prep for tomatoes. Pat dry. Marinate 30 min in honey mixture.

Lemon Infusion

Marinate
30 min

[4 servings]
10 oz (300 g) cherry tomatoes · Juice of 1 lemon · ½ tsp salt · 2 tsp soy sauce · 1 Tbsp Brown sugar · 2 Tbsp olive oil · Coarsely grated pepper · Thin quarter slices lemon

1. Peel tomatoes (Basic Prep); pat dry. Marinate in other ingredients 30 min.

Radishes

- Basic Prep:
Slice and rub with salt; or use as is
- Also Try in:
salt-rubbed Plum Vinegared (p. 48)
thinly sliced Green Tea (p. 40)

Garlic Miso

Marinate 30+ min

‖ [4 servings] 20 radishes with tops · 2 Tbsp miso · ½
‖ tsp crushed garlic

1. Combine the miso and garlic.
2. Cut off radish tails and cut a deep X into each root
end.
3. Stuff Xs with miso mixture (fig). Let stand 30-60 min, keeping leaves away from miso.

Shiso Berries

Marinate 30 min

[4 servings] 20 radishes ·
1-2 Tbsp salt-preserved shiso
berries (shiso no mi no
shiozuke)

1. Slice radishes into
⅕ in-thick (5 mm) rounds.
2. Combine with shiso in
plastic bag. Tie bag; let stand
30 min (fig).

Apricot Syrup

Marinate 30+ min

‖ [4 servings] 20 radishes · ⅔
‖ tsp salt · 2 Tbsp apricot
‖ jam · 2 Tbsp vinegar

1. Cut radishes in half.
Sprinkle with the salt. Let
stand 30 min.
2. Combine jam and vinegar
in a bowl.
3. Pat radishes dry. Let stand
in jam mixture 30+ min.

Green Beans

- **Basic Prep:**
  Blanch, then cool in a colander
- **Also Try in:**
  blanched Curry Pickles (p. 43)
  grilled or broiled Grilled (p. 20)

Soy Sauce with Jako

Marinate 1 hr

[4 servings] 10 oz (300 g) green beans · 3 Tbsp chirimenjako (tiny sardines) · 4 Tbsp sake · 2 tsp mirin · 3 Tbsp soy sauce

1. Blanch beans. Spread in a colander to cool.
2. Boil jako, sake, and mirin briefly. Cool and add soy sauce.
3. Halve beans crosswise. Place in plastic bag. Pour jako mixture over. Tie bag; let stand 1 hr.

Misozuke

Marinate 2 hrs

[4 servings] 7 oz (200 g) green beans · 20-30 shiso leaves · ¾ cup miso · 1½ tbsp mirin

1. Blanch beans. Cool. Pat dry.
2. Combine miso and mirin.
3. Halve beans. Wrap 3 bean pieces in 2 shiso leaves (*fig 1*); repeat.
4. Following steps on page 5, layer: plastic wrap, half of miso, paper towel, all beans, paper towel (*fig 2*), rest of miso. Close wrap. Let stand in a plastic bag 2-3 hrs. Slice diagonally.

White Wine and Dill

Marinate 1+hrs

[4 servings] 7 oz (200 g) green beans · Dill weed · ⅓ cup white wine · 3 Tbsp sugar · 1½ tsp salt · 5 Tbsp vinegar

1. Choose thin beans. Blanch and cool.
2. Boil dill, wine, sugar, and salt briefly. Cool and add vinegar.
3. Put beans in a wide-mouthed jar. Let stand in wine mixture 1+ hours.

Japanese Peppers	•Basic Prep: Rub with salt; or sauté. •Also Try in: salt-rubbed Sweet Vinegar (p. 26)

Simply Ginger

Marinate 1 hr

‖ [4 servings] 30 Japanese peppers (shishito) · 1 knob
‖ ginger, julienned · 1 tsp salt

1. Make vertical slits in the peppers to aid flavor
absorption.
2. Combine ginger and
peppers in a plastic bag.
Add the salt (fig) and let
soften (5-10 min). Press air
out of bag, tie bag, and let
stand 1 hour.

Soy Sauce

Marinate Til cool

‖ [4 servings] 30 Japanese peppers (shishito) · 2 Tbsp
‖ cooking oil · 2 Tbsp sake · 1 Tbsp mirin · 3 Tbsp soy
‖ sauce · ⅕ oz (5 g) shaved bonito

1. Slice peppers in half. Sauté over high heat in the oil.
Add sake and mirin. Remove from heat.

2. Stir in soy sauce and bonito. Let cool.

Myoga	•Basic Prep: Myoga are Japanese ginger flowers. Rub with salt or rinse with boiling water. •Also Try in: salt-rubbed Sweet Vinegar (p. 26)

Misozuke

Marinate 2+hrs

‖ [4 servings] 12 myoga · ¾ cup miso · 1-½ Tbsp mirin

1. Slice myoga in half lengthwise. Mix miso and mirin
thoroughly.
2. As shown on p. 5, layer: plastic wrap, half of miso
mixture, paper towel, myoga, paper towel, remaining
miso. Let stand 2+ hours.

Okra

- **Basic Prep:**
Rub off the fuzz with salt (*fig*), then either sauté or blanch and cool.

- **Also Try in:**
blanched Wasabi Soy Sauce (p. 11)

Lemon Sauté

Marinate — Til cool

[4 servings] 40 okra · Salt for rubbing · 2 Tbsp olive oil · ¼ onion, thinly sliced · 1½ Tbsp vinegar · 1½ Tbsp lemon juice · 2 tsp sugar · 1½ tsp salt · Dash pepper

1. Rub off the fuzz with the salt. Rinse off and pat dry. Remove stems. Slice in half diagonally.
2. Sauté okra briefly in the oil. Soak okra in remaining ingredients til cool.

Ginger Miso

Marinate — 2 hrs

[4 servings] 20 okra · Salt for rubbing · ¾ cup miso · 1½ tsp grated ginger · 1½ Tbsp mirin

1. Rub off okra fuzz with salt. Blanch okra; cool. Mix ginger, miso, and mirin.
2. As on p. 5, layer: plastic wrap, half miso, paper towel, okra, paper towel, remaining miso. Seal in plastic 2 hrs.

Kabocha

- **Basic Prep:**
Deep fry or blanch.
- **Also Try in:**
fried Parsley Crisp (p. 37)

Honey Fry

Marinate — Til cool

[4 servings] ¼ kabocha squash · Cooking oil · Pinch salt · 2-3 Tbsp honey

1. Cut kabocha to bite size and peel. Deep fry until soft at 340°F (170°C). Drain. Add salt. Fold honey in. Let stand til cool.

Ginger

- Basic Prep:
Sprinkle with salt (*fig*) and rub; or rinse in boiling water.
- Also Try in:
rinsed Misozuke (p. 24)

Sweet Vinegar

Marinate
30 + min

‖ 2 knobs ginger • 1 tsp salt • 6 Tbsp vinegar • 3 Tbsp
‖ sugar • 2 Tbsp mirin

1. Peel ginger and slice very thin. Sprinkle with salt and
let stand to soften. Squeeze well.
2. Marinate in vinegar-sugar-mirin mixture 30 min.
Keeps 10 days, chilled. (Serve with sushi.)

[Vinegared Ginger Stalks]
A special Sweet Vinegar technique with
young ginger stalks. Scrape any dirt from the
ginger and rinse. Dip the root ends in boiling
water, then place in a glass of 4 Tbsp
vinegar, 3 Tbsp sugar, 2 Tbsp mirin ½ tsp
salt for 1 hr (*fig*). Delicious as a garnish for
grilled fish.

Honey Lemon

Marinate
30 min

‖ 3 knobs ginger • ¼ lb (100 g) honey • ¼ cup lemon
‖ juice

1. Peel ginger and slice thin. Rinse with boiling water.
Drain. Let stand in honey-lemon mixture 30 min. Keeps
10+ days, chilled.

Cooking with Tsukemono

● Using Honey Lemon Ginger

Ginger Ale

[1 serving] 3 Tbsp
Honey Lemon Ginger
syrup • 120-150 cc soda
water, chilled

1. Pour the soda over
the syrup in a glass.
Add some of the ginger
if desired.

Jellied Ginger Ale

[2 servings] 2 tsp gelatin
powder • 3 Tbsp cold water • ½
cup Honey Lemon Ginger syrup •
6-7 slices Honey Lemon Ginger

1. Sprinkle gelatin over the cold
water. Chill 10-15 min. Add ¼
cup water and cook in microwave
1 min. When gelatin melts, add ¾
cup water and the syrup.

2. Mince 1 slice ginger for
garnish. Place others in cup with
gelatin mixture. Chill til firm.

Garlic

- Basic Prep:
Use raw.
- Also Try in:
Sweet Vinegar (opposite); Misozuke (p. 35); Garlic Chile Oil (p. 63)

Honey Vinegar

Marinate
1/2 + day

|| [about 1 cup] 1 head garlic · 5 Tbsp vinegar · 1 Tbsp
honey · ½ tsp salt

1. Mince the garlic.
2. Mix vinegar, honey, and salt well. Place in jar with
garlic and let stand ½ day or more.
* Use in dressings, marinades, and steak sauce. After 1
day, refrigerate to avoid fermentation. Keeps 2 weeks.

Kombu Soy Sauce

Marinate
1 day

|| [about 1 cup]
1 head garlic · 1-2 dried red chiles · 10 cm kombu · ½
cup soy sauce · 3 Tbsp boiled sake

1. Peel garlic cloves. Halve lengthwise and remove
cores. Halve and seed pepper(s). Cut kombu with
scissors into ⅓ in (1 cm) widths.
2. Let ingredients stand in a jar 1 day. Keeps in
refrigerator 2 weeks or more.
* Use in chow mein, in fried rice, or as a sauce for tofu
salad.

Cooking with Tsukemono

● using Honey-Vinegar Garlic

Garlic Dressing

[2 servings] 1½ Tbsp
Honey-Vinegar Garlic (with
marinade) · 3 Tbsp olive oil · ⅓
tsp salt · Dash pepper

1. Combine all
ingredients.
2. Serve on
your favorite
vegetables.

● using Kombu Soy Sauce Garlic

Yaki Udon

[2 servings] 3 oz (100 g) sliced
pork · Salt and pepper · 4 Tbsp
Kombu Soy Sauce marinade, plus
1 piece of the garlic · ½ carrot ·
2 leaves cabbage · 2 packages
precooked udon noodles · 3 Tbsp
cooking oil

1. Salt and pepper the pork.
2. Thinly slice garlic and carrot.

Chop cabbage. Loosen udon with
boiling water.
3. Stir-fry pork and vegetables.
Stir in udon. Flavor
with marinade.

Premade Nuka to the Rescue!

Never-Fail Speedy Nukazuke

Making traditional nuka-doko–a pickling base made with rice bran (*nuka*), seasonings, and vegetable cuttings–takes 2-3 weeks. Also, temperature changes can affect the fermentation, giving unpredictable results for beginners. Instead, we use commercially available pre-made nuka, adding our own flavorings for terrific, speedy, and delicious results.

● Nuka-Doko in Stores

Premade nuka is sold in plastic containers or in sealed bags, in the refrigerated section of Japanese specialty markets.

1 Prepare the Nuka-Doko

Place kombu strips into the nuka. Add other flavorings as desired (right).

Ingredients for
Nuka-Doko 1 pack
pre-made nuka-doko
Kombu

● Flavor Enhancers for Nuka-Doko

Dried chiles   Soybeans   Dry mustard   Cracked sansho peppercorns

* Also try dried shiitake or surume (dried squid)

2 Add Vegetables

Marinate 6-24 hrs

Cucumbers

Place untrimmed cucumbers in the nuka. To speed the process, rub well with salt.

Marinate 1-2 days

Japanese eggplant

Remove leaf-like coverings from stem end. To speed the pickling, sprinkle with salt first.

Marinate 1-2 days

Carrots

Halve lengthwise. Cut to fit container. Can be peeled or not, as desired.

Marinate 1-2 days

Turnips

Trim tops, leaving 1 in (3 cm) on. Cut a deep X into the bottom end. Stuff nuka in the opening.

Marinate 1-2 days

Cabbage

Cut to fit container. Insert some nuka between every few leaves.

Marinate ½-1 day

Myoga (Japanese ginger)

Trim off roots and add to nuka.

* Pickling times are shorter in summer, longer in winter. Experiment with different times.

More Speedy Nukazuke Vegetables

Marinate 1-2 days

Daikon

Cut to fit container, then peel. Quarter lengthwise (if thin, halve lengthwise).

Marinate ½ day

Edamame

Boil until not quite tender. Pat dry. Place in netting, then add to nuka-doko.

Marinate ½-1 day

Celery

Devein the celery. Cut to fit container.

Marinate ½ day

Broccoli

Cut into flowerets. Boil until not quite tender to speed pickling. Add to nuka-doko.

Marinate 6 hrs

Udo

Cut to fit container. Peel.

Marinate 1 day

Cauliflower

As for broccoli, cut into flowerets and boil until not quite tender.

Marinate 6-24 hrs

Bell Pepper

Halve lengthwise. Remove stem and seeds.

Marinate 1 day

Lotus Root

Peel. Slice into ⅓ in (1 cm)-thick quarter rounds. Boil until not quite tender.

Marinate 6-24 hrs

Japanese Peppers

Cut off the stem. For easy removal, place in netting before adding to the nuka-doko.

Marinate 1 day

Ginger

Cut into smallish pieces. Peel and add to the nuka-doko.

Nukazuke Q & A

Q1. What maintenance is needed?

A. Every day (twice a day in summer) stir well from the bottom, folding air in. This stirring prevents souring or molding. After stirring, flatten the surface and wipe the sides. Also, as the nukadoko is used again and again, replenish it with more nuka and salt.

Q3. How can soured nukadoko be restored?

A. When the nukadoko over-ferments, it grows sour. Remove all vegetables. Add dry mustard. Stir well twice a day for 2-3 days before adding vegetables.

Q2. How can watery nukadoko be thickened?

A. Juicy vegetables will make the nukadoko too watery. Place several changes of paper towels on top. Or make a well with a cup, then use a paper towel to absorb the liquid that pools up.

Q4. What to do about long trips away from home?

A. Remove all vegetables. Flatten the surface and wipe the container. Add toasted nuka (rice bran). Sprinkle with sliced dried chile peppers and salt. Place in refrigerator. Remove the salt layer before using again.

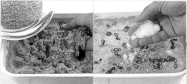

Cooking with Tsukemono

● using Nukazuke

Chicken-Nukazuke Medley

[2 servings] 3 oz (100 g) skinless chicken breast · 3 tsp sake · ¼ tsp salt · 1 tsp cornstarch · 3 oz (100 g) Nukazuke pickles, any variety or combination · ½ naganegi (Japanese bunching onion) or white part of 2-3 scallions · ½ dried chile, seeded · 1½ Tbsp cooking oil · ½ tsp sesame oil

1. Slice chicken at an angle into small strips. Rub with 1 tsp of the sake and the salt. Add cornstarch and toss well.
2. Thinly slice the nukazuke. Thinly slice the naganegi on the diagonal.
3. Cook the chicken in 1 Tbsp of the oil until browned. Remove.

4. Cook the nukazuke, naganegi, and chile in remaining oil. Return chicken to pan. Sprinkle with remaining sake. Add sesame oil just before serving.

● using Over-Pickled Nukazuke

Ginger-Bonito

[2 servings] 5 oz (150 g) over-pickled nukazuke · 1 knob ginger, julienned · 2-3 Tbsp shaved bonito · 2-3 tsp roasted sesame seeds · Soy sauce to taste

1. Slice nukazuke. Soak in water to remove salt. When just a hint of salt is left, squeeze well.
2. Combine nukazuke, ginger, bonito, and sesame seeds. Season with soy sauce.

Eggplant

·Basic Prep:
Rub with salt or pan-fry to remove bitterness.

·Also Try in:
pan-fried Spicy-Sweet Style (p. 9); Dashi-Soy
Sauce (p. 34); Kimchee Style (p. 47)

Shiso Squeeze

Marinate 10 min

[4 servings] 5 Japanese eggplants · 2 tsp salt · 10
leaves shiso · 2 myoga (Japanese ginger) · 1 Tbsp
roasted sesame seeds

1. Slice eggplants into ⅛ in-thick (3 mm) rounds.
Sprinkle with the salt
immediately (*fig*), then
toss. Soften 1-2 min.
Squeeze out the liquid
completely.
2. Julienne the shiso.
Chop the myoga.
3. Combine all
ingredients. Let stand 10
min.

Sesame Vinegar

Marinate 2 hrs

[4 servings] 5 Japanese eggplants · 3 Tbsp ground
sesame seeds (white) · 2 Tbsp sugar · 2 Tbsp soy
sauce · 2 Tbsp vinegar · 1 tsp grated ginger · 5-6
Tbsp cooking oil

1. Mix sesame and sugar well. Stir in vinegar and soy
sauce a little at a time. Add ginger.
2. Slice eggplants into ½ in (1.5 cm) rounds. Brown
both sides in the oil (*fig 1*).
3. When soft, drain oil. Toss in the sesame mixture
(*fig 2*). Cool, then chill thoroughly, around 2 hrs.

Spicy Soy Sauce

Marinate 10 min

[4 servings] 5 Japanese eggplants · 1 tsp salt · 2 tsp
prepared Oriental mustard (neri-karashi) · 1½ Tbsp
soy sauce · 2 tsp mirin

1. Cut eggplant into ¾ in (2 cm) dice. Stir in the salt.
Let stand 15-30 min.
2. Combine remaining
ingredients well.
3. Squeeze eggplant well
and toss in the mustard
mixture. Let stand 10-15
min.

Ume Vinegar

Marinate 10 min

[4 servings] 5 Japanese eggplants · 1½ tsp salt · 1
Tbsp mirin · 1 Tbsp sugar · 2-3 Tbsp vinegar · 2
umeboshi (pickled plums), seeded

1. Chop eggplants. Stir in the salt and let stand 15-20
min.
2. Combine mirin, sugar, and vinegar. Add minced
umeboshi (*fig 1*).
3. Squeeze eggplant well and toss in ume mixture.
Let stand 10-15 min.

Clockwise from top right:
Spicy soy Sauce, Ume Vinegar, Sesame Vinegar, shiso Squeeze

Mushrooms

- Basic Prep:
Sauté; grill; or blanch
- Also Try in:
grilled Roasted (p. 12)
blanched Curry Pickles (p. 43)

Miso Vinegar

Marinate
Til cool

[4 servings] 2 packs shimeji mushrooms, in stalks · 12 fresh shiitake, thinly sliced · 3 Tbsp vinegar · 4 Tbsp miso · 2 Tbsp mirin · 1 Tbsp sugar · 3 Tbsp cooking oil

1. Mix vinegar, miso, sugar, and mirin.
2. Sauté the mushrooms in the oil until wilted. Add to miso mixture. Let cool.

Tarragon Vinaigrette

Marinate
Til cool

[4 servings] 8 button mushrooms · 2 packs shimeji mushrooms · 1 pack enoki mushrooms · ½-1 bay leaf · ½ stalk fresh tarragon · 1 Tbsp vinegar · 2 Tbsp lemon juice · 2 tsp sugar · 1 tsp salt · Dash pepper

1. Halve button mushrooms lengthwise. Separate shimeji stalks. Remove enoki base, cut stalks in half, and separate.

2. Mix other ingredients.
3. Put mushrooms, shimeji, and enoki into plenty of boiling water, pausing between each ingredient. Drain immediately after adding enoki.
4. Shake water off well. Stir into vinaigrette. Let cool.

Dashi Soy Sauce

Marinate
Til cool

[4 servings] 10 oz (300 g) maitake mushrooms · ½ cup dashi stock (see note on p. 3) · ¼ cup mirin · ½ cup soy sauce

1. Boil dashi and mirin just to cook off the alcohol. When cool, add soy sauce.
2. Separate maitake into large chunks. Sear quickly over high flame.

3. Add hot maitake to remaining ingredients. Let cool.

Yamaimo

Nagaimo

Yamatoimo

- Basic Prep:
Peel and use raw. Taro root is a good substitution for both varieties.

- Also Try in:
in matchsticks Shiso Berries (p. 22)
deep fried Fried Style (p. 10)

Soy Sauce Marinade

Marinate
1 hr

[4 servings] 10 oz (300 g) fresh yamatoimo, peeled · ¼ cup soy sauce · 2 Tbsp mirin · Aonori (nori sprinkles)

1. Cut yamatoimo into 2 in (5 cm) sticks.
2. Combine soy sauce and mirin.
3. Put yamatoimo in plastic bag with the liquid. Tie bag and let stand 1-2 hrs.
4. Drain. Sprinkle with nori.

Misozuke

Marinate
1 hr

[4 servings] ¾ lb (350 g) fresh nagaimo · ⅔ cup miso · 2 tsp mirin · Shiso leaves

1. Peel nagaimo and halve lengthwise.
2. Blend mirin into miso.
3. Put nagaimo in a plastic bag, spreading miso mixture between the pieces (*fig 1*). Let stand 1-2 hrs (*fig 2*).
4. Wipe off miso and slice.
Serve on shiso leaves.

Cooking with Tsukemono

● using Dashi Soy Sauce Mushrooms

Ume-Mushroom Fried Rice

[2 servings] ¼ lb (100 g) Dashi Soy Sauce Mushrooms · 2 umeboshi (pickled plums) · ¼ lb (100 g) hot cooked rice · 1 egg, beaten · 4-5 scallions · 3 Tbsp cooking oil

1. Mince the Mushrooms. Shred the umeboshi. Chop the green onions.
2. Heat the oil and lightly scramble the eggs. Add the rice and stir.

3. When rice is dry, stir in maitake and umeboshi. Add green onions at end.

Carrot

- Basic Prep:
  Blanch; sauté lightly; or use raw.
- Also Try in:
  sautéed Lemon Sauté (p. 25)
  halved lengthwise Misozuke (p. 35)

Orange-Mint Ribbons

Marinate Til cool

‖ [4 servings] 2 carrots, peeled · 3 Tbsp raisins · 3 Tbsp
‖ olive oil · 4 Tbsp orange juice · 1 Tbsp vinegar · ½ tsp
‖ salt · 1 sprig mint, chopped

1. Rinse raisins in warm water; drain.
2. Combine liquids and salt.
3. Make carrot ribbons with peeler (*fig 1*). In a strainer, submerge in boiling water several seconds. Drain. Add to dressing with raisins and mint (*fig 2*).
4. Let cool. Garnish with mint sprig.

Miso Sauté

Marinate Til cool

‖ [4 servings] 2 carrots · 4 Tbsp miso · 2 Tbsp mirin · 1
‖ Tbsp sugar · 2 Tbsp cooking oil

1. Peel carrots and chop in thin pieces.
2. Combine miso, mirin, and sugar.
3. Sauté briefly over high heat. Toss in miso mixture.

Let cool.
* Wait 1 hr for deeper flavor.

Cuttlefish Soy

Marinate 1 hr

‖ [4 servings] 2 carrots · ¾ oz surume (dried
‖ cuttlefish) · ½ cup hot water · 3 Tbsp
‖ mirin · 4 Tbsp soy sauce

1. Cut surume into thin strips with scissors and soak in the water 30 min. Cut carrots into 2 in matchsticks.
2. Place all ingredients including soaking water in plastic bag (*fig*). Let stand 1 hr.

Potatoes

- Basic Prep:
Deep fry; or boil briefly.
- Also Try in:
quick-boiled Kimchee Style (p. 47)
deep fried Worcestershire (p. 39)

Parsley Crisp

Marinate Til cool

[4 servings] 3 potatoes • 1 Tbsp minced onion • 1 Tbsp minced parsley • Crushed garlic • 2 tsp dry mustard • 2 tsp sugar • 2 tsp soy sauce • 1 Tbsp vinegar • 3 Tbsp olive oil • Cooking oil

1. Peel and dice the potatoes (½ in; 1.5 cm). Soak in water.
2. Combine next 8 ingredients.
3. Pat potatoes dry. Deep fry in 340°F (170°C) oil. When heated through and crisp, drain well.
4. Add to marinade while hot (*fig*). Let cool at room temperature.

Cooking with Tsukemono

⬤using Orange-Mint Ribbons

Carrot Sandwiches

[4 servings] 5¼ oz (150 g) Carrot Ribbons • 4 soft rolls • 3 oz (80 g) cream cheese • Fresh mint
1. Stir cream cheese to soften.
2. Slit the rolls. Insert cream cheese and welldrained carrot ribbons. Garnish with mint.

Vinegared Julienne

Marinate Til cool

[4 servings] 3 potatoes • 1½ Tbsp vinegar • 1½ tsp mirin • 1½ tsp sugar • ½ tsp salt • Black roasted sesame seeds

1. Mix vinegar, sugar, mirin, and salt.
2. Peel potatoes, julienne, and soak in water. Rinse well. Using a strainer, place in boiling water and stir quickly (*fig*). Remove at once. Drain well.
3. Combine with vinegar mixture. Cool.
4. Garnish with sesame seeds.

Gobo

•Basic Prep:
Boil briefly.

•Also Try in:
boiled Sweet Vinegared (p. 46)
boiled Soy Sauce Vinegar (p. 47)

Wine Marinade

Marinate
1 hr

[4 servings] 7 oz (200 g) young gobo (burdock root) • 1 dried chile pepper • 3 Tbsp sugar • 3 Tbsp white wine • 1 tsp salt • ½ tsp peppercorns • 3 Tbsp vinegar plus more for soaking

1. Wash gobo well. Cut into short lengths. Halve or quarter lengthwise. Soak in vinegared water. Halve and seed the chile.
2. Pour a bit of vinegar into boiling water. Boil gobo until al dente.
3. Boil sugar, wine, salt, peppercorns, chile. Cool and add the vinegar and the gobo. Let stand about 1 hr.

Sesame Miso

Marinate
1 hr

[4 servings] 10 oz (300 g) gobo (burdock root) • ¾ cup miso • 1 Tbsp mirin • 2-3 Tbsp ground sesame seeds

1. Wash gobo well. Cut to fit pot; boil. When softened, drain. Pound with wooden pestle (*fig 1*) to crack surface.
2. Stir mirin and sesame into miso.
3. On plastic wrap, spread half of miso, then gobo, then

remaining miso. Seal in wrap. Let stand in plastic bag 1-2 hrs.
4. Wipe miso off. Cut to serving length.

Cooking with Tsukemono

●using Sesame Miso Gobo **Chicken-Gobo Patties**

[2-3 servings] 7 oz (200 g) finely ground chicken • 1 Tbsp sake • ½ beaten egg • ¼ lb (100 g) Sesame Miso Gobo • 2-3 scallions, white part only • 2 Tbsp cornstarch • Black sesame seeds to taste • 3 Tbsp cooking oil

1. Mix chilled chicken, sake, and beaten egg until slightly sticky.
2. Add shredded Gobo, minced scallions, and cornstarch.
3. Form into 4 patties. Put sesame seeds in center. Fry on both sides in the oil until crisp.

Worcestershire

Marinate
Til cool

[4 servings] 10 oz (300 g) lotus root · ⅓ cup worcestershire sauce · 3 Tbsp preboiled sake · 1 clove garlic · 3 Tbsp olive oil

1. Peel lotus root; dice (¾ in; 2 cm). Soak in water. Chop garlic (2-4 pcs).
2. Combine worcestershire and sake.
3. Fry lotus root and garlic in the oil until crisp. Stir into sauce while hot. Let cool.

Lotus Root

·Basic Prep:
Soak in water or vinegared water, then boil or sauté.
·Also Try in:
boiled Wasabi Soy Sauce (p. 11)
deep-fried or sautéed Fried Style (p. 10)

Sweet Vinegar

Marinate
Til cool

[4 servings] 10 oz (300 g) lotus root · 2 in (5 cm) kombu · ½ cup water · ½ dried chile pepper · 2 Tbsp sake · 2 Tbsp mirin · 3 Tbsp sugar · 1 tsp sugar · ½ cup vinegar plus more for soaking

1. Julienne kombu with scissors. Soak in the water. Seed chile and slice.
2. Boil sake and mirin briefly. Dissolve sugar and salt in mixture. Add the vinegar and soy sauce.
3. Peel lotus root. Slice in thin rounds. Soak in vinegared water.
4. Add a dash of vinegar to boiling water. Boil lotus root slices briefly.
5. Drain well. Soak in sake mixture (*fig*) until cool.

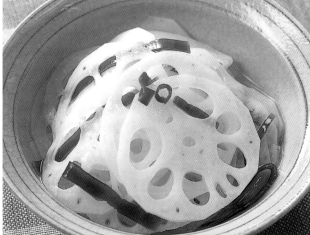

Nambanzuke

Marinate
Til cool

[4 servings] 10 oz (300 g) lotus root · 1 naganegi or 2-3 scallions, sliced diagonally · 1 dried chile, seeded · 3 Tbsp sake · 2 Tbsp mirin · 2 Tbsp sugar · ½ cup dashi stock (see note on p. 3) · ¼ cup vinegar · ¼ cup soy sauce · Cooking oil

1. Peel the lotus root. Slice into ¼ in-thick (7 mm) half rounds. Pat dry.
2. Briefly boil the chile, sake, mirin, and sugar. Add the vinegar and soy sauce.
3. Sauté the lotus root in plenty of oil. Add the naganegi/scallions.
4. When lotus root is soft, remove contents of pan, drain on a rack, and add to the sake mixture. Let cool.

Daikon

- Basic Prep:
Slice and use raw; air dry; or rub with salt.
- Also Try in:
salt-rubbed Kombu-zuke (p. 14)
Apricot Syrup (p. 22) Kombu Mix (p. 44)

Citron Infusion

Marinate 1 hr

[4 servings] 14 oz (400 g) daikon · 2 tsp salt · Zest from ½ citron, julienned · 2 tsp citron juice · 3 Tbsp sugar · 4 Tbsp vinegar · 1 Tbsp mirin

1. Cut daikon to 2 in (5 cm) sticks. Add salt. Keep in plastic bag 30 min (fig 1).
2. Combine remaining ingredients.
3. Squeeze daikon. Place in a plastic bag with marinade. Let stand 1 hr.

Chinese Style

Marinate 1 hr

[4 servings] 14 oz (400 g) daikon · 50 g dried apricots · 1 Tbsp Chinese rice wine · ¼ cup soy sauce · 1 Tbsp sugar · 1 Tbsp sesame oil

1. Dice daikon (½ in; 1.5 cm). Air-dry on a rack ½ day in fresh air (fig 1, 2).
2. Chop apricots into 4-6 pieces each. Microwave with sherry 30 sec. Add remaining ingredients.
3. Let daikon and marinade stand in plastic bag 1+ hrs.

Soy Sauce

Marinate 1 hr

[4 servings] 14 oz (400 g) daikon · 4 in (10 cm) kombu · ⅓ cup soy sauce · 2 Tbsp mirin

1. Dice kombu (⅓ in; 1 cm). Mix with soy sauce and mirin. Let stand.
2. Peel daikon. Halve lengthwise. Finely score the outer sides, diagonally (fig 1).
3. Put in plastic bag with marinade. Let stand 1 hr, inverting occasionally

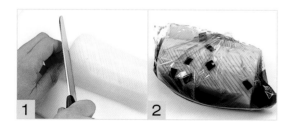

Green Tea

Marinate 20 min

[4 servings] 14 oz (400 g) daikon · ½ dried chile · 2 tsp green tea leaves (sencha) · 1⅓ tsp salt

1. Slice daikon into 2-in (5-cm) matchsticks. Seed and slice chile.
2. Shake all ingredients together in a plastic bag to combine.
3. When soft, squeeze tightly, tie off, and let stand 20 min.

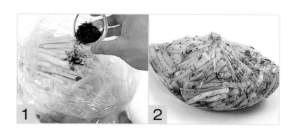

clockwise from top right:Chinese Style, Green Tea, Soy Sauce, Citron Infusion

Broccoli

- **Basic Prep:**
Break into florets. Rinse
with boiling water (*fig*).
To use stems, peel and
slice thin. Or, blanch or
deep fry.
- **Also Try in:**
hot-rinsed Citron
Kombu, Curry Pickles,
Yukari (opposite); Sweet Vinegar (p. 39)

Spicy Soy

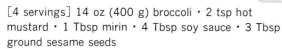

**Marinate
30 min**

[4 servings] 14 oz (400 g) broccoli · 2 tsp hot
mustard · 1 Tbsp mirin · 4 Tbsp soy sauce · 3 Tbsp
ground sesame seeds

1. Break broccoli into florets and rinse with boiling
water as above.
2. Mix mirin in mustard; add soy sauce.
3. Put broccoli and mustard mixture in bag. Let stand
30+ min. Add sesame.

Asazuke

**Marinate
1 hr**

[4 servings] 14 oz (400 g)
broccoli · 1 apple · 1 Tbsp
sugar · 1 Tbsp lemon juice ·
1½ tsp salt · 4 Tbsp water

1. Prepare broccoli as above.
Cool.

2. Core apple. Cut in fans
with peel on.
3. Mix remaining ingredients.
Mix well in plastic bag with
broccoli and apple. Let stand
1 hr.

Kombu Tea Fry

**Marinate
Til cool**

[4 servings] 14 oz (400 g)
broccoli · 1 Tbsp kombu tea
granules · 3 Tbsp water · 2
Tbsp preboiled sake · ½
naganegi or white part of 2
scallions, coarsely chopped ·
Dash coarsely ground
pepper · Cooking oil

1. Dissolve kombu tea in the
water and sake. Add the
naganegi and pepper.
2. Separate broccoli into
florets. Deep fry at 360°F
(180°C).
3. Drain and combine with
other ingredients while hot.
Let cool.
* Note: If kombu tea does not
dissolve, heat it, then add
pepper and naganegi after it
has cooled.

Cauliflower

- Basic Prep:
Same as broccoli (opposite)
- Also Try in:
hot-rinsed Tarragon Vinaigrette (p. 34)
Spicy Soy (opposite)

Citron Kombu

Marinate
1 hr

[4 servings] 1 small cauliflower · Zest from ½ citron · 2 tsp citron juice · 4 Tbsp soy sauce · 1 Tbsp mirin · 4 in (10 cm) kombu · 2 Tbsp preboiled sake

1. Julienne the kombu with scissors. Soak in the sake. Julienne the zest.
2. Cut cauliflower and rinse as above.
3. Drain. Mix with all ingredients. Let stand 1 hr, stirring occasionally.

Curry Pickles

Marinate
Til cool

[4 servings] 2 tsp curry powder · 2 Tbsp sugar · 2 Tbsp white wine · 1 tsp salt · 3 Tbsp vinegar · 3 Tbsp olive oil · 1 clove garlic, halved · 1 small cauliflower

1. Combine first 6 ingredients. Add garlic.

2. Break cauliflower into florets. Blanch. Drain well and fold into curry mixture. Let stand til cool.

Yukari

Marinate
Til cool

[4 servings] 2 large umeboshi · 1-2 Tbsp yukari (salted dried beefsteak leaves) · 2 Tbsp mirin · 1 Tbsp each sugar, vinegar, water · 1 small cauliflower

1. Seed the umeboshi and mince. Mix with next 5 ingredients.
2. Break cauliflower into florets and blanch. Drain well. Add to marinade and toss.

Serve when cool.
*Note: If yukari is too salty, use less.

43

Hakusai

•Basic Prep:
Rub with salt or sauté briefly.

•Also Try in:
salt-rubbed Salt-Sesame (p. 12), Honey Apple
(p. 20), Shiso Squeeze (p. 33)

Kimchee

Marinate
1 hr

|| [4 servings] 14 oz (400 g) hakusai · 1½ tsp salt · ½
bunch nira (Japanese scallion) · 1 Tbsp kochujang
(Korean spicy bean paste) · 2 tsp soy sauce

1. Chop hakusai. Soften with the salt in plastic bag
15-20 min. Squeeze out all liquid. Cut nira in 1 in
(3 cm) lengths.
2. Put hakusai and nira in a
bag with mixed soy sauce
and kochujan (fig 1).
3. Knead mixture well
through opening of the bag.
Seal and let stand 1 hr.

Kombu Mix

Marinate
1 hr

|| [4 servings] 14 oz (400 g) hakusai · 4 in (10 cm)
kombu · Citron zest, sliced thin · 2 tsp salt

1. Trim hakusai leaves from stalks. Chop leaves
coarsely. Cut stalks to bite size.
2. Julienne the kombu with scissors.
3. Place chopped stems in plastic bag with the salt
(fig 1). Let soften 5 min.
4. Add remaining ingredients (fig 2). Shake bag and
let stand. When softened, squeeze all air out of bag
and tie (fig 3). Let stand 1 hr.

1 2 3

Labaicai (Spicy Chinese Style)

Marinate
1 hr

|| [4 servings] 10 oz (300 g) hakusai stems · 2 Tbsp
sugar · 1 tsp salt · 4 Tbsp vinegar · 1 Tbsp sake · 3
Tbsp sesame oil · 1-2 tsp Sichuan peppercorns

1. Cut hakusai into 2 in (5 cm) slabs.
2. Mix next 4 ingredients in a big bowl.
3. In the oil, cook the peppercorns over low heat until
fragrant. Raise heat and add hakusai stems just to
coat in oil.
4. Toss in marinade while hot (fig). Let stand 1 hr.

* Notes: Do not overcook
hakusai. Sichuan
peppercorns (huajiao) can
be substituted with
powdered sansho.

Sweet Vinegar

Marinate
1 hr

|| [4 servings] ¾ lb (350 g) hakusai stems · 1¾ oz (50
g) carrot · 1 knob ginger, julienned · 1 tsp salt · 2
Tbsp sugar · 2 Tbsp soy sauce · 4 Tbsp vinegar

1. Cut carrots into bite-sized slabs. Cut hakusai into
slightly larger slabs. Soften carrots, hakusai, and
ginger in a plastic bag with the salt 20-30 min (fig 1).
2. Squeeze. Return to bag with rest of ingredients.
Seal. Rest 1-2 hrs (fig 2).

1 2

Clockwise from top right: Labaicai,
Sweet Vinegar, Kombu Mix, Kimchee Style

Naganegi

•Basic Prep:
Grill; or blanch, then marinate while hot.

•Also Try in:
blanched Lemon Sauté (p. 13)
Soy Sauce with Jako (p. 23)

*Note:Naganegi (Japanese bunching onion) is similar to leeks.

Grilled

Marinate
Til cool

[4 servings] 3 naganegi • 4 in (10 cm) kombu • 3 fl oz
(70 cc) boiling water • 2 Tbsp sake • 2 Tbsp mirin • 4
Tbsp soy sauce

1. Cut kombu small; soak in the water.
2. Boil kombu with water; add sake and mirin; boil.
Remove. Add soy sauce.
3. Chop naganegi into 1 in (3 cm) lengths. Grill or broil
until just browned.
4. Add, still hot, to liquids. Let cool.

Sweet Vinegar

Marinate
Til cool

[4 servings] 3 naganegi • 1 pack shimeji mushrooms •
1 Tbsp sugar • 1 Tbsp lemon juice • 1 tsp salt • 2 Tbsp
vinegar

1. Slice naganegi into 1½ in (4 cm) half rounds.
Separate shimeji.
2. Put naganegi in plenty of boiling water, pause, then
add shimeji. Drain.
3. While hot, toss in marinade. Cool.

Dried Daikon

•Basic Prep:
Rinse strips. Soak in water 10-20 min. Squeeze out gently to preserve flavor.

•Also Try in:
Soy Sauce with Jako (p. 23) Squid Soy Sauce (p. 36)

Hariharizuke

Marinate
1 hr

[4 servings] 3 oz (80 g) dried daikon strips • 4 in (10
cm) kombu • 3 Tbsp boiling water • 1 knob ginger • 1
dried chile pepper • 3 Tbsp vinegar • 3 Tbsp sake • 5
Tbsp soy sauce

1. Prepare daikon as described above. Chop. Julienne
ginger.
2. Cut kombu into thin strips and soak in the water.
Seed chile; cut into rounds.
3. Combine all ingredients. Let rest 1 hr.

Bean Sprouts

- Basic Prep:
Wash, drain, then boil
briefly (*fig*) until bean
portion softens.
- Also Try in:
boiled Sweet Vinegar (p. 37)

Soy Sauce Bonito

Marinate
Til cool

[4 servings] 10 oz (300 g) bean sprouts · 2 Tbsp
sake · 4 Tbsp boiling water · ⅙ oz (5 g) shaved
bonito · 4 Tbsp soy sauce · 1 knob ginger, julienned

1. Boil sake in the water. Add bonito; let cool. Add soy
sauce and ginger.
2. Prepare bean sprouts as above. Drain. Add to
marinade while hot. Cool.

Kimchee Style

Marinate
Til cool

[4 servings] ⅛ tsp crushed garlic · ⅛ tsp crushed
ginger · ½ tsp mustard powder or a dash of cayenne · 2
tsp sugar · 2 tsp vinegar · 2½ tsp soy sauce · 2 Tbsp
sesame oil · 10 oz (300 g) bean sprouts · 1 Tbsp
roasted sesame seeds · 4-5 scallions, chopped

1. Combine first 7 ingredients in bowl.
2. Prepare sprouts as shown above.
3. Toss hot sprouts in marinade. Let cool. Garnish with

scallions and sesame.

Cooking with Tsukemono

●With Soy Sauce Bonito Bean
Sprouts

Okinawa Style

[4 servings] 3-5 oz (100-150 g)
Soy Sauce Bonito Bean Sprouts ·
1 block medium-firm tofu (11 oz;
300 g) · 1¾ oz (50 g) minced
pork · ¼ bunch nira (Japanese
scallion) · 2 eggs · ½ tsp salt ·
4 Tbsp cooking oil

1. Wrap tofu in paper towels.
Weigh down to press out liquid.
Chop nira.
2. Heat 3 Tbsp of the oil in a
wok. Add tofu, breaking it up
coarsely by hand. Add salt.
Stir-fry til browned. Remove.
3. Add remaining oil to wok.
Stir-fry pork, then stir in Bean
Sprouts, then return tofu to wok,
then add nira.

4. Drizzle beaten egg into mixture
from upper edge of wok. Stir and
serve.

Turnips

- **Basic Prep:**
  Rub with salt to encourage flavor absorption.
- **Also Try in:**
  salt-rubbed Kombu style (p. 14), Kombu Mix (p. 44)
  raw Garlic Misozuke (p. 22) Soy Sauce; Chinese Style (p. 40)

Acharazuke

Marinate 1+ hr

|| [4 servings] 14 oz (400 g) turnips · 1 tsp salt · 2 oz (60 g) dried persimmons · 1 dried chile pepper · 4-5 Tbsp vinegar

1. Peel turnips and cut into 2 in (5 cm) sticks. Sprinkle with the salt. Soften 10-15 min, then squeeze out all liquid.
2. Julienne persimmons. Seed the chile.
3. Combine persimmons, vinegar (*fig*), and chile in a bowl.
4. Add turnips to bowl. Let stand 1+ hr.

Note: Any tsukemono made with sweetened vinegar and chile is called Acharazuke. Here, persimmons supply the sweetness.

Basic Salt

Marinate 1 hr

|| [4 servings] 14 oz (400 g) turnips · 1¾ oz (50 g) turnip greens · 1½ tsp salt

1. Peel turnips. Halve lengthwise and slice thin. Chop greens (use tender, center leaves).
2. Shake turnips, greens, and salt in plastic bag (*fig 1*). Let stand 10-15 min.
3. When soft, knead by hand. Press air out of bag; tie; let stand 1 hr (*fig 2*).

Senmaizuke

Marinate 2 hrs

|| [4 servings] 3 large turnips · 4 in (10 cm) kombu · 2 Tbsp vinegar · 3 Tbsp mirin · 2 tsp salt

1. Julienne kombu with scissors. Soak in vinegar 30+ min; add mirin. Peel turnips and slice on a mandoline (*fig 1*).
2. In a bowl, layer some turnip, salt, kombu. Repeat layers (*fig 2*), ending with turnip and remaining salt (*fig 3*).
3. Put plastic wrap atop. Press 2-3 hrs with a plate and cans (*fig 4*). Slice.

Plum Vinegared

Marinate 2 hrs

|| [4 servings] 1¼ lbs (500 g) turnips · ½ tsp salt · ⅓ cup plum vinegar · 2-3 Tbsp sugar

1. Peel turnips and slice into wedges. Place in plastic bag with salt 30 min.
2. Mix vinegar, sugar.
3. When turnips are soft, squeeze out. Return to bag with vinegar mixture (*fig*). Close bag; let stand 2-3 hrs.

From top:Acharazuke, Senmaizuke, Basic Salt, Plum Vinegared

Seri
(Japanese Parsley)

- Basic Prep:
Trim roots; arrange in a colander and rinse with boiling water (*fig*).
- Also Try in:
Kombu-Wrapped (p. 10), Spicy Soy (p. 42)

Chopped

Marinate
30 min

‖ [6 servings] 10 oz (300 g) seri · 1 tsp salt · 1 oz (30 g) reconstituted wakame

1. Rinse seri in boiling water. Cool. Cut into 1 in (3 cm) pieces. Chop wakame.
2. Shake with salt in plastic bag. Knead through opening. Seal for 30 min.

Dashi-Soy

Marinate
30 min

‖ [4 servings] 7 oz (200 g) seri · 1 Tbsp powdered bonito · ½ cup water · 2 tsp mirin · 1 Tbsp soy sauce · 2 Tbsp roasted sesame seeds

1. Rinse seri in boiling water. Cool.
2. Boil water, salt, mirin. Add bonito. Remove from heat and add soy sauce.
3. Marinate seri in soy mixture with the sesame seeds 30 min, then chop.

Mizuna

- Basic Prep:
Knead with salt. (Mizuna are similar to dandelion greens.)

- Also Try in:
salt-rubbed Salt-Sesame (p. 12)
raw Tosa-Style (p. 7)

Chopped

Marinate
1 hr

‖ [4 servings] 10 oz (300 g) mizuna · 4 in (10 cm) kombu · ½ dried red chile, seeded · ⅔ tsp salt

1. Cut mizuna in 1 in (3 cm) lengths.
2. Julienne kombu with scissors.
3. Shake mizuna, kombu, chile, and salt in a plastic bag. Let soften 10-15 min. Squeeze out the air; tie; let stand 1 hr.

Kiku no hana
(Chrysanthemum petals)

• Basic Prep:
Drop a handful of petals into boiling vinegar water. Drain, plunge in cold water, and drain well.

• Also Try in:
Soy Sauce Bonito (p. 47)
Misozuke (p. 23)

Plum Vinegared and Vinegared

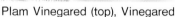

Marinate
30 + min

[4 servings] 5¼ oz (150 g) purple chrysanthemum petals • ½ tsp salt • 2 tsp umeboshi flesh • 2 tsp vinegar • 1 Tbsp mirin [for yellow petals, omit umeboshi and mirin; use ⅔ tsp salt and 1 Tbsp vinegar]

1. Combine everything except petals.
2. Prepare petals as described above. Toss in marinade and let stand 30+ min.

Plam Vinegared (top), Vinegared

Cooking with Tsukemono

● using Yellow Vinegared Tsukemono

Tricolor Tsukemono

[4 servings] ¼ lb (100 g) Vinegared chrysanthemum tsukemono • 6 fresh shiitake mushrooms • Dash salt • 2 cucumbers • 2 tsp salt • 1 Tbsp vinegar • 1 Tbsp mirin • 2 tsp sugar • Dash salt • 1 tsp soy sauce • Roasted sesame seeds

1. Grill shiitake, top side down. Sprinkle with salt and julienne.
2. Slice cucumbers into thin rounds. Sprinkle with 2 tsp salt and soften 5-10 min. Squeeze.
3. Combine remaining ingredients. Arrange cucumbers, chrysanthemum, and shiitake, then pour liquid over.

● using Plum Vinegared Chrysanthemum

Daikon-Chrysanthemum

[2 servings] ¼ lb (100 g) Plum Vinegared chrysanthemum with liquid • 1 cup grated daikon

1. Press out liquid from daikon. Toss with chrysanthemum.

Simple Tsukemono with Canned Beans

Marinate Beans

Marinate
1 hr

[4 servings] 8½ oz canned mixed beans • 4 Tbsp minced onion • 1 Tbsp minced parsley • 3 Tbsp catsup • 3 Tbsp olive oil • 1 Tbsp lemon juice • 1 Tbsp red wine • 2 tsp soy sauce • Dash each of salt, pepper, chili powder

1. Combine everything except beans.
2. Stir liquid into beans. Chill 1 hr.

Cooking with Savory Foods

Certain foods are said in Japanese to have umami, a savory quality. Special dried or pickled ingredients lend a depth and intensity to tsukemono.

With dried squid

Marinated Squid

Marinate
2 hrs

[4 servings]
2½ oz (70 g) smoked squid
1 onion
1 rib celery
2-3 slices lemon

¼ cup lemon juice
½ cup cooking oil
2 tsp soy sauce
Dash pepper

1. Thinly slice onion and celery. Mix liquids and pepper, then add squid and lemon. Let stand 2 hrs.

With dried shrimp

Carrots with Shrimp

Marinate
30 min

[4 servings]
⅓ oz (10 g) dried shrimp
7 oz (200 g) carrots
½ tsp salt

1. Halve carrots crosswise. Cut thin strips with a peeler. Mix with shrimp and salt in a plastic bag. Tie. Let stand 30 min.

With zhacai pickles

Cucumber and Chinese pickles

Marinate
1 hr

[4 servings]
1½ oz (40 g) zhacai, Chinese pickles

10 oz (300 g) cucumbers
1 Tbsp sesame oil

1. Thinly slice zhacai. Slice cucumbers in ⅛ in (3-4 mm) diagonal rounds. Mix in plastic bag; add oil. Close for 1 hr.

With salted cherry blossoms

Turnips and Cherry Blossoms

Marinate
30 min

[4 servings]
⅓ oz (10 g) salted
cherry blossoms   14 oz (400 g) turnips

1. Peel turnips. Slice into thin rounds.
2. Shake salt from blossoms. Chop.
3. Combine in a plastic bag. Shake well. Press out air; tie. Let stand 30 min.

With salted kombu

Daikon with Salted Kombu

Marinate
30 min

[4 servings]
1 oz (30 g) salted   14 oz (400 g) daikon
kombu (choose a brand   Daikon leaves
that is not too salty)

1. Cut daikon into 1½ in (5 cm) slabs. Mince leaves. Julienne kombu with scissors.
2. Combine all in plastic bag. Shake well. Press out air; tie. Let stand 30 min.

With sweet-pickled shallots

Vegetable Medley

Marinate
1 hr

¼ lb (100 g) carrots
5¼ oz (150 g) turnips
¼ lb (100 g) cucumbers
1 tsp salt   (pickled shallots), with ⅕
3 oz (80 g) rakkyo   cup (50 ml) of its liquid

1. Quarter carrots; cut ⅓ in (1 cm) thick. Cucumbers, turnips: a bit bigger.
2. Mix with salt in bag. Let rest 30 min.
3. Squeeze well. Return to bag with thinly sliced rakkyo and liquid. Tie and let stand 1 hr.

Fruit, Seafood, Meats

Tsukemono is not just for vegetables.
Expand your repertoire with these
make-ahead desserts
and main courses.

Strawberries in Wine Syrup

Marinate 6+ hrs

Keeps for: 2-3 days

1

Rinse strawberries with tops still on. Pat dry. Remove tops. Halve small fruit; quarter large ones.

1¼ lbs (600 g) strawberries
10 oz (300 g) honey
½ cup white wine

2

Thoroughly mix honey and wine in a bowl.

3

Place strawberries in a jar. Let stand 6 hrs. To keep longer, transfer to a refrigerator.

Note: try plums, apricots, or dried prunes instead of strawberries.

Cooking with Strawberries in Wine Syrup

Strawberry Sorbet

[4 servings]
10½ oz Strawberries in Wine Syrup
¾ cup to 1 cup water

1. Combine all ingredients in a metal dish (*fig 1*). Freeze 2-3 hrs.
2. Break up with a fork and puree in a food processor (*fig 2*).
3. When mixture is whitish and fluffy (*fig 3*), return to dish (*fig 4*); freeze 1 hr.

Strawberry Float

[2 servings] ½ cup syrup from Strawberries in Wine Syrup 1 cup soda 2 scoops vanilla ice cream Strawberries to taste

1. Divide Strawberries among two glasses. Add Syrup.
2. Pour chilled soda into glasses (*fig*). Float ice cream on top.

Raisins in Rum Syrup

9 oz (250 g) raisins
1¾ oz (50 g) golden raisins
3½ oz (100 g) prunes

5¼ oz (150 g) sugar
¾ cup (150 cc) water
4 fl oz (120 cc) rum

Marinate Til cool

Keeps for: 1+ month

1 Boil water and sugar. Cool and add rum.

2 Rinse both kinds of raisins in warm water. Stir into plenty of boiling water. Drain.

3 Chop prunes and place in jar with hot raisins and syrup. Let cool.

Cooking with Raisins in Rum Syrup

Cupcakes

[14 cupcakes] 7 oz (200 g) fruit from Raisins in Rum Syrup, squeezed dry • ¼ lb (100 g) unsalted butter • 5¼ oz (150 g) brown sugar • 2 eggs • 5¼ oz (150 g) pastry flour • 1½ tsp baking powder • 1¾ oz sliced almonds

1. Cream butter (softened) with brown sugar until fluffy.
2. Beat in 1 egg. Mix flour and baking powder in another bowl; stir half into egg mixture.
3. Beat remaining egg and stir in gently.
4. Sprinkle with remaining flour mixture. Add Raisins and mix well.
5. Pour into paper-lined muffin tins. Sprinkle with almonds. Bake 20 minutes in top rack of a 360°F (180°C) oven. Cool. To store, wrap tightly in plastic wrap.

Sabayon

[4 servings] ¾ syrup from Raisins in Rum Syrup • 4 brioches • ½ cup hot water • 1/2 cup whipping cream • 3-4 Tbsp fruit from Raisins in Rum Syrup

1. Slice off the tops of the brioches. Wrap in aluminum foil. Heat through in a toaster oven. Arrange in a baking dish.
2. Combine syrup and hot water. Cook 2 minutes in a microwave. While brioches are still hot, pour syrup into the cut openings (fig), soaking completely.
3. Chill. Serve with whipped cream and fruit.

Cupcakes (top), Sabayon

Honeyed Oranges

14 oz (400 g) navel
oranges
7 oz (200 g) honey

1 Wash oranges with hot
water. Slice the zest
from 2 of the oranges.

2 Trim peel and membranes
from all oranges. Slice
sections from membranes
as shown.

3

Marinate ½ day

Keeps for: 2-3 days

Place sections and zest in a jar.
Add honey and let stand for a half
day. Keeps up to 3 days in
refrigerator.

Cooking with Honeyed Oranges

Orange Jelly

[4 servings] 2 tsp powdered
gelatin · 3 Tbsp cold water · ¾
cup syrup from Honeyed Oranges ·
1¼ cup water · Several sections
from Honeyed Oranges

1. Sprinkle gelatin over the cold
water. Chill 10-15 min. Mix syrup
and water.
2. Cook gelatin mixture in
microwave 30 sec-1 min to dissolve.
3. Stir gelatin mixture into syrup.
Pour over orange sections in 4
glasses.
4. Chill until firm.

Baked Orange
Cheesecake

[2 cakes in 4½ x 7 in oval dishes]
4½ oz (120 g) cream cheese · 1 oz
(30 g) honey · 2 oz (60 g) sour
cream · 1 egg yolk · ½ beaten
eggs · 2 Tbsp almond powder · 1
Tbsp pastry flour ·

14-15 orange sections from
Honeyed Oranges

1. Stir honey, sour cream, egg yolk,
and beaten egg (in that order) into
softened cream cheese.
2. Stir in almond and flour. Spread
in 2 buttered oval baking dishes.
Smooth tops. Pat orange sections
dry and place atop. Place on
rimmed baking sheet.
3. Pour hot water into baking sheet.
Bake 40-50 min in 320°F (160°C)
oven.

Grilled Squid

Marinate
1 hr

[4 servings]
2 squid bodies
2 Tbsp mirin
3 Tbsp soy sauce

1 tsp liquid from grated
ginger

1 Place a resealable bag in a bowl (to prevent spills). Add all liquid ingredients.

2 Peel and open the squid. Score diagonally. Cut into 2 ½ in squares. Add to bag.

3 Seal bag. Chill 1-2 hrs.

How to cook

Heat a burner-top grill over low heat. Pat dry. Grill quickly on both sides.

Miso Scallops

Marinate
1/2 day

[4 servings]
12 large sashimi-grade
scallops

⅔ cup miso
½ cup sake lees paste

1 Mix miso and sake lees. (If paste is unavailable, crumble pressed lees; add sake. Let soften overnight.)

2 Spread half of miso on wrap. Top with paper towel scallops.

3 Fold towel over, Spread with remaining miso.

4 Close wrap. Chill in a plastic bag ½ day.

How to cook

Grill quickly on a heated grill.

Chicken Crisps

Marinate 1 hr

[4 servings]
1¼ lbs (500 g) chicken thigh meat
¼ cup red wine
¼ cup soy sauce
2 Tbsp honey

1
Cut chicken in bite-sized pieces. Place in bag with other ingredients.

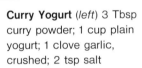

2
Seal bag and chill 1-2 hrs.

Other Chicken Marinades

Curry Yogurt (*left*) 3 Tbsp curry powder; 1 cup plain yogurt; 1 clove garlic, crushed; 2 tsp salt

Thai Sauce (*right*) 2 Tbsp nam praa (Thai fish sauce); 1 clove garlic, crushed; 3 Tbsp sake

How to cook

Pat dry. Dredge in cornstarch. Deep fry until crisp in 340°F (170°C).

Miso-Garlic Pork

Marinate 2 hrs

[4 servings]
4 pork cutlets
1 clove garlic, crushed
⅔ cup miso
3 Tbsp mirin
2 Tbsp sake

1
Trim the pork. Combine all other ingredients.

2
Place a bit of miso mixture in a bag. Add one cutlet. Alternating with more miso, layer remaining cutlets in bag.

3
3. Top with remaining miso. Tie bag and chill 2-6 hrs.

* If pork will marinate longer than 6 hrs, reduce miso to ½ cup and increase sake 4 Tbsp-less salt.

How to cook

Wipe off miso. Sauté in a little oil.

Spiced Red Snapper

Marinate
2 hrs

[4 servings]
4 pieces red snapper
2 tsp coarse salt
½ tsp sliced dried chile
Dash coarsely ground pepper
Fresh basil and thyme
1 Tbsp sake
4 Tbsp cooking oil

1 Tear basil and thyme by hand. Combine with all spices and liquids in a dish.

2 Coat snapper in marinade. Chill 2 hrs.

How to cook

Sauté in a little oil until crisp on both sides and cooked through.

Mayonnaise Shrimp

Marinate
1 hr

[4 servings]
10 oz (300 g) shrimp
1 Tbsp soy sauce
5 Tbsp mayonnaise

1 Mix soy sauce and mayonnaise in a large bowl.

2 Rinse shrimp. Peel and devein, leaving tails on. Chill in mayonnaise mixture 1-2 hrs.

Other Shrimp Marinades

Sesame Mayonnaise Mix 4 Tbsp mayonnaise, 2 Tbsp ground sesame seeds, and 2 Tbsp miso.

Onion Sauce Mix 3 Tbsp each grated onions, minced parsley, and vegetable oil; 1 tsp salt; and coarsely ground pepper.

How to cook

Scrape off the marinade. Sauté in a heated pan.

Chicken Nanbanzuke

 Marinate Til cool

[4 servings]
1¼ lbs (500 g) chicken thigh meat
½ tsp salt
½ Tbsp sake
Pastry flour for dredging
Cooking oil
½ cup mirin
½ cup dashi

1 Tbsp sugar
1-2 dried chile peppers
1 naganegi or white part of 3 scallions
1 large knob ginger
¼ cup vinegar
½ cup soy sauce

1 Boil mirin. Add dashi, sugar, and halved, seeded chile(s). Boil briefly.

2 Transfer to a dish. Add sliced naganegi, thinly sliced ginger, vinegar and soy sauce.

3 Dice chicken. Knead with salt and sake; let stand 10-15 min. Dredge in flour. Deep fry at 340°F(170°C). Cool in naganegi mixture.

Seared Beef

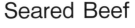 Marinate 2+hrs

[4 servings]
1¼ lbs beef
½ tsp salt
2 Tbsp cooking oil
½ cup dashi (see p. 3)
4 Tbsp mirin
5 Tbsp soy sauce
Juice from 2 limes
2-3 lime slices

1 Let beef come to room temperature. Rub with the salt.

2 Heat a frying pan. Add the oil. Sear the beef on all sides and put in a dish.

3 Mix remaining ingredients and pour over beef. Marinate 2-3 hrs, turning occasionally. *Drape with a paper towel to prevent drying out.

*Slice and serve with chopped scallions.

Herb Vinegars, Oils, Honeys

Infuse vinegars, oils, and honeys with the flavors of your favorite herbs and spices. Keep several types on hand for salads, marinades, and more. Store in a cool, dark place.

Basil Oil

2½ cups oil
1½ oz (40 g) basil

1. Pat basil dry. Add to oil; keep1 day or more.

■ Keeps for: 1 month

Uses

● **Pasta**
For 4 servings, heat sliced dried chile peppers in 8 Tbsp Basil Oil. Add 1½ lbs clams and ½ cup white wine. When shells open, toss with cooked spaghetti (¾ lb dried).

● **Marinated seafood**
For 4 servings, combine ⅔ cup Basil Oil, 3 Tbsp vinegar and 3 Tbsp lemon juice, 1 tsp sugar, 1 Tsp salt, 2 tsp soy sauce, dash pepper, 14 oz steamed seafood, 4-5 Tbsp liquid from steaming.

* Also can be used for omelets and pilaf.

Mint Honey

1¼ lbs honey
1 handful mint

■ Keeps for: 1 month

1. Pat mint leaves dry. Add to honey; keep 1 day.

Uses

● **Lemonade**
For 1 serving, mix 2 Tbsp Mint Honey with 1 Tbsp lemon juice and ¾ cup chilled soda. Serve with ice and lemon slices.

● **Hot Milk**
Pour heated milk in a cup. Add Honey Mint to taste.

* Also delicious with plain yogurt or on grapefruit.

62

Herbed Vinegar

2½ cups vinegar
2 bay leaves
2-3 parsley stems
1 sprig thyme
2-3 sprigs tarragon

2-3 dried chile peppers
2-3 cloves garlic
2 tsp peppercorns

1. Seed the chiles. Halve and core the garlic.
2. Mix all ingredients. Keep half day.

■ Keeps for:
   2-3 weeks

Uses

●**Dressing**
For 4 servings, mix 2 Tbsp Herbed Vinegar with 4 Tbsp vegetable oil, ½ tsp salt, and a dash of pepper. Serve on your favorite salad.

●**Sauce for Fried Foods**
Drizzle instead of lemon juice over fried chicken, breaded shrimp, and other deep-fried foods. The herbs add a fresh flavor.

* Also try on potato salad, in pickle marinade, and on pasta salad.

Garlic Chile Oil

2½ cups olive oil
5 dried chile peppers
5 cloves garlic

1. Seed the chiles. Halve and core the garlic. Place in oil ½ day or more.

* Also use on chilled Chinese noodles or Thai-style salads.

■ Keeps for: 1 month

Uses

●**Garlic Bread**
Brush on baguette slices. Bake until golden in a toaster oven. Sprinkle with minced parsley.

●**Boiled Pork Marinade**
For 4 servings, mix 3 Tbsp Garlic Chile Oil, 1 Tbsp vinegar, 1 Tbsp mirin, 2 Tbsp soy sauce. Pour over 10 oz (300 g) boiled pork. Serve with sliced scallions.

Dill Oil

2½ cups vegetable oil
1-2 sprigs dill

1. Pat dill dry. Place in oil. Marinate 1 day or more.

- Keeps for:
  1 month

Uses

●**Sautéed Smelt**
Lightly salt and pepper 4-5 smelt. Sauté on both sides in 3-4 Tbsp Dill Oil.

●**Sautéed Potatoes**
Slice 4 potatoes and sauté with minced bacon in 3-4 Tbsp Dill Oil.

* Also use to sauté chicken or seafood for pasta.

Rosemary Honey

1¼ lb (500 g) honey
1 large sprig rosemary

1. Pat rosemary dry. Place in honey. Wait 1 day or more.

- Keeps for:
  1 month

Uses

●**Cream Cheese Spread**
Mix Rosemary Honey into cream cheese, a perfect base for the fragrance of the rosemary and the sweetness of the honey.

●**Pork Sauce**
For 4 servings, crush 1 clove garlic and heat in 1 Tbsp oil. Reduce balsamic vinegar to ⅓ volume and add to pan, with 1 Tbsp Rosemary Honey, 2 tsp soy sauce, and salt and pepper. Swirl in 6 Tbsp butter. Pour over sautéed pork.

* Drizzle on buttered toast; swirl into compotes; add a hint to tomato salads.

64